Brendan the Navigator

Winner of the Bisto Book of the Decade Award
(With *Exploring the Book of Kells*)

'A perfect book ... Simms has shone his craftsman's light of love on
the world of Brendan and made it live'
The RTE Guide

'A new interpretation and explanation by a leading scholar'
The Leinster Leader

D0817081

GEORGE OTTO SIMMS was born in Dublin in 1910. He took his BA, MA, BD, PhD and DD degrees at Trinity College, Dublin. Ordained a priest of the Church of Ireland in 1936, he spent his working life in the service of the Church and was Archbishop of Dublin from 1956 until 1969, and then Archbishop of Armagh and Primate of All Ireland from 1969 until his retirement in 1980. A respected scholar and historian, he lectured and wrote extensively, particularly on the Book of Kells, on which he was internationally recognised as an expert. For almost forty years he contributed a weekly religious feature, 'Thinking Aloud', to *The Irish Times*. *Exploring the Book of Kells* was Dr Simms's first book for younger readers, it received wide acclaim and won the Reading Association of Ireland Award. *Brendan the Navigator, Exploring the Ancient World* was his second book for children; it was also critically acclaimed and, together with *Exploring the Book of Kells*, was joint winner of the Bisto Book of the Decade Award. Dr Simms also wrote *Saint Patrick, Ireland's Patron Saint*. George Otto Simms died in 1991.

BRENDAN
THE
NAVIGATOR
EXPLORING THE ANCIENT WORLD

GEORGE OTTO SIMMS

Drawings
DAVID ROONEY

THE O'BRIEN PRESS
DUBLIN

This revised edition first published 2006 by The O'Brien Press, Ltd.,
20 Victoria Road, Dublin 6, Ireland.
Tel: +353 1 4923333; Fax: +353 1 4922777
E-mail: books@obrien.ie
Website: www.obrien.ie
First published 1989. First published in paperback 1990.
Reprinted 1993, 1997. Revised 2006.

ISBN-10: 0-86278-960-5
ISBN-13: 978-0-86278-960-2

Copyright © The O'Brien Press Ltd.

All rights reserved. No part of this book may be reproduced or
utilised in any way or by any means, electronic or mechanical,
including photocopying, recording or by any information storage
or retrieval system without permission in writing from the
publisher.

British Library Cataloguing in Publication Data
Simms, George Otto, 1910-
Brendan the navigator. - 2nd ed.
1. Brendan, Saint, the Voyager, ca. 483-577
2.Brendan, Saint, the Voyager, ca. 483-577 - Legends
3.Christian saints - Ireland - Biography
I. Title
282'.092

5 6 7 8 9 10
06 07 08 09 10

Editing, layout, design and typesetting: The O'Brien Press
Drawings: David Rooney
Printing: MPG Books Ltd

PICTURE CREDITS AND ACKNOWLEDGEMENTS
The publisher wishes to thank the following for permission to reproduce images.
Front cover: Tim Severin's boat used in his 'Brendan Voyage' courtesy of the
Tim Severin Archive. **Back cover**: stone carving of St Brendan, Bantry, Co. Cork,
courtesy of the Irish Image Collection. **Inside**: photographs, p 17, Des Lavelle,
from *The Skellig Story, Ancient Monastic Outpost* (O'Brien Press). The quotation
from Robin Flower is from *The Western Island*, Oxford University Press, 1944.

Contents

A twelfth-century picture of Brendan's ship alongside Jasconius, the friendly whale.

CHAPTER 1

Brendan:
A Warm-hearted Saint

'From small beginnings out to undiscovered ends'
Hilaire Belloc

BRENDAN WAS AN IRISH PERSONALITY who became a legend and a world-figure. Many who have never visited Ireland look up to Brendan and claim him as their own man. This hero, teacher, traveller, leader, and saint is well known in a host of countries. The story of his great journey in search of his 'Treasure Island' has been told in many languages – Dutch, German, French, Italian, Spanish as well as in English, and, of course, in Irish!

He is admired, not for his possessions, but for his character. His treasure was not gold or silver or sparkling jewellery. He did not even have great herds of cattle like the

wealthy farmers of his day. Yet he was gifted. The riches
that he possessed were given to him by God.

Brendan's gifts included his courage, his faith, his
vision, his love of people, his inspired leadership, his skills
in seamanship, his compassion, his cheerfulness and, we
might add, his sense of humour. He used these graces to
the full. The list is long in a life that was crammed with
action and exciting adventures spent in God's service.
This made him both happy and popular.

BIRTH

A bright light shone in Kerry on the day that Brendan was
born. Bishop Erc tells us of his vision. He baptised the baby
born to Findlung and his wife in the year A.D. 483 (or 484).
Brendan's mother had a vision, too, when this happy
event took place. She had a feeling that someone of great
good fortune had come into the world. Like the bishop,
she perceived that a bright future lay before baby Brendan.

BRENDAN'S HOMELAND

Barra, the place of Brendan's birth, was by the sea-shore as
you travel from Tralee to Fenit Head. From Tralee Bay, a
wonderful view stretches southwards and out to the west.
Great mountains sweep down to the sea on that part of the
Dingle peninsula. Caherconree rises like a strong fortress,
keeping guard over the lower slopes of its towering
height. Seen from Fenit and from further north, its peak
stands out in the Slieve Mish mountain range that
stretches west to Beenoskee and on to Mount Brandon, the
highest summit, which bears Brendan's name. Rising ma-

Brendan's story told in the Dutch language five hundred years ago.

jestically about one thousand metres above Brandon strand and sea level, this hill of Brandon, Brandon creek and Brandon point have been landmarks through many centuries, guiding seafarers, sailors and fishing crews, when the storms come and the mists hover over the coastline.

The view from Brandon's top on a clear day stretches east and south over more mountains and deep valleys. Lakes and streams gleam in the sunlight amid the brown bog-land and stony foothills. Westerly from this height is a grand panorama from the jagged, rocky points of the Three Sisters, to the Blasket Islands, further south to the Skelligs and endlessly out to the wide horizons of the ocean. The mighty Atlantic invites adventure, exploration and new discoveries. Many who 'go down to the sea in ships, and occupy their business in great waters' have been challenged by the vastness of the great deep. They have been fascinated, too, by the mystery that lies beyond the horizon, far exceeding the range of any human eye.

In such surroundings, Brendan was born. His first year was spent with the sound of the sea and of the churning waves in his ears. A wild beauty and some of Ireland's most majestic scenery surrounded his birthplace.

EDUCATION – WITH ITA AND ERC

However, this saint-in-the-making who in later life was always 'on the move' spent his next few years, from the age of two until he was five, in Killeedy near Newcastle West in county Limerick. Here he was fostered by the famous St Ita (or Íde) who cared for the young in a very special way.

This is Brendan's sea, and yonder Brendan's mountain, cloud-encompassed,
stands lonely in the sky.
*Mount Brandon, the highest peak in the mountain range that stretches along the Dingle
peninsula in Kerry, rises majestically from the water. Beyond, and further to the west,
lie the Blasket Islands and the broad Atlantic Ocean.*

The training, the feeding, the teaching and the learning about Jesus Christ prepared the child for life and shaped his character for a future still to be unfolded.

It is thought that Brendan kept in touch with his foster-mother, Ita, in later years. The impression which she made upon him lasted long. He did not forget her. Indeed, Ita was called 'the foster-mother of the saints of Ireland'. Many interesting personalities were brought to her and we can guess how important was her influence from the following story told about Brendan.

It was said that Brendan asked Ita what were the three things that God specially loved. The answer came from Ita:

God loves a true faith in Him with a pure heart;
a simple life with a religious spirit;
and open-handedness inspired by charity.

This story helps us to see something of Ita's outlook and way of life. We can understand why her words were popular, and often repeated among the people, who saw these three spiritual treasures shining out of the life and work of Brendan, when he had grown up.

At the age of five, Brendan left Killeedy, and Bishop Erc, who had plans for the child's future, brought him back to the homeland of his parents. Erc was now in charge of Brendan's education and began to teach him more fully about the Christian faith. Termon Eirc (Erc's Sanctuary) is the name of a townland near Ardfert, a short distance

A nature book, dated 1475, shows all sorts of fishy creatures filling the sea. These are the creatures later fifteenth-century artists thought Brendan saw on his journey across the Atlantic.

north from Fenit.

Years later, when Brendan was ordained, he was given Ardfert monastery to look after. A well in Ardfert is called after him, and the name of Brendan is affectionately remembered in many ways among the people of Kerry. He had been, as a child, a neighbour among the local families. This was Brendan country.

OTHER TEACHERS

Plans for Brendan's great voyage into
unknown seas are discussed.

Changes had to come in Brendan's life. Erc wished him to have other teachers at a time when there was little organised school life. For this reason, Brendan's travels began and he was sent to have further education with St

Jarlath of Tuam, a well-known tutor. While he was with this teacher in Galway, he seems to have travelled further north through Mayo. We picture him gaining wider experience of Ireland, visiting families in their homes, and sharing his faith and learning with those whom he met.

Another teacher to whom Brendan owed much was the distinguished Enda whose monastery was on Inishmore, the largest of the three Aran islands in Galway Bay. Enda had been a soldier in his youth, but when he felt called to train for the Christian ministry he found a wise guide and fine teacher in Scotland. This was St Ninian who lived at Whithorn, Galloway, across the narrow channel that separates Ireland from Scotland.

Enda was anxious to find a quiet spot for prayer and study and the life of spiritual discipline. To his great joy, he was granted the kind of place, 'away from it all', that he was hoping for. It was to be called 'Aran of the Saints' after Enda had trained many Christian leaders who in turn founded monasteries in different parts of Ireland. These were built on the same lines as Enda's centre of prayer, study and farm-work on Inishmore.

Brendan was to become one of those outstanding Christian leaders of the early Irish Church. From his teachers he learned the power of prayer and showed a deep and caring love for people. With the example of Erc, Ita, Jarlath and Enda to inspire him through life, he continued the strong tradition of prayer, study and practical Christianity for which the Irish monasteries were to become famous, far beyond the island of Brendan's birth.

CHAPTER 2

Irish Christian Monasteries

I N THE CENTURIES AFTER ST PATRICK, who is said to have died in the year A.D. 461, many monasteries were founded throughout Ireland. Two of these are particularly associated with Brendan. In the year A.D. 558 he founded a monastery near the river Shannon at Clonfert, in what is now county Galway, and he returned there after his famous voyage. Ardfert in Kerry also holds many memories of his birth and early life.

Clonfert in Brendan's time may have been surrounded by a wall of stone. This would have provided protection for the buildings inside and would have kept out wild or even domestic animals. Robbers and invaders would not easily have made an unobserved entrance. Dry stones, not held together by mortar, were probably used to make a stout defence. Judging by the unmortared walls of the monastery of Inishmurray island off the Sligo coast, these

Above: More than 160 metres above the Atlantic, six stone huts where monks lived and a small church are perched on the summit of Skellig Michael.
Below: The beehive huts and stone crosses at the monastic settlement on Skellig Michael are a testament to the profound devotion of the monks.

walls might have been from two to five metres in thickness, and perhaps four metres high. The buildings of the monastery where Brendan lived would have been of wood. Even the church was probably not built of stone and was certainly very different from the present Clonfert Cathedral with its magnificently carved doorway in the west wall, which dates from the twelfth century. We can in our imagination catch a glimpse of the difficult days which faced Clonfert when we read that between the mid-seventh century and the late twelfth century, the monastery suffered burnings and plunderings no fewer than nine times.

Some Irish monasteries were quite small. For example, on the highest point of Skellig Michael, about 160 metres above the sea, a church was perched on the cliff. Some cells of stone, shaped like beehives, clustered round, and the marks left by stone pegs for hanging up book-satchels can be traced on the wall. Food was very simple. Most meals were of fish and greenery. Goats who grazed on the slopes of the island rock would have supplied the community with milk. A vegetarian diet was part of the rule of life in the monastery.

Other monasteries, such as Clonfert and Ardfert, were large enough to be looked on as 'cities'. The abbey would have owned many fields surrounding the monastic buildings, so there would be a farm to look after. Apart from the life of prayer and silence, schools were organised for the education of the neighbourhood. A scriptorium or writing room was necessary for the writing of books and the copying of the scriptures. A monastery was called a 'city', since very many people known as *manaigh* settled nearby with their families to help the monks in the management of the farm, the keeping of bees, the planting and growing of trees. These *manaigh* were lay-persons, often married, whose children benefited from the schooling given by the community. They worked for the monastery and in return received the care of the Church.

There were various kinds of monks in the history of the Christian Church. Some were called hermits, while others lived together in a 'monastic family', as a community, sharing their life of prayer, study, and practical work.

Long ago hermits lived lonely lives in the sands of Egypt, away from other people. They did not dislike the human race, but they wanted to be alone with God. They were not really lonely, because they felt that they were near to God in a special way. They found that God was the best company they had ever enjoyed.

Ireland also had its hermits, and there are many stories about the strange lives which they led. Some of the ideas for this kind of alone-ness probably came from the Middle East. People who had gone as pilgrims to the Holy Land often brought back eastern customs and began to follow them when they came home again to Ireland. Many place-names in Ireland, for example Desertcreat in County Tyrone and Desertmartin in County Donegal, remind us of these 'deserted' spots. Hermits lived a hard life, sleeping in the open, and eating the simplest kinds of food.

But the more usual life of the monk was spent in groups. A few like-minded monks would share a community life together, living with a special rule of prayer and work to

Brendan visits Enda on the island monastery of Aran
to learn more about the monastic way of life.

guide them in planning their day. They were sometimes called a 'monastic family' with an abbot, as a father-figure, in charge of the monastery and its life. Columba, from the island of Iona, kept in touch with many foundations which bore his name, as their abbot; his personality had a great influence on all who belonged to his widely scattered 'family' of monks. In the same way, Brendan, as abbot, was closely associated with Ardfert and very specially with Clonfert.

ATHLETES OF GOD

The monks or nuns who lived in communities followed a rule of life, with prayers being offered throughout the day and night. There were rules also about the kind of food which they ate at their meals. It was a strict and simple life. There were times of fasting, but there was feasting too when the community celebrated the Christian festivals as they came round each year.

The monks promised to obey the abbot who was in charge. The members of the community received instructions about the various duties which had to be carried out and they would be punished quite severely if they failed in these duties. It was a strict life, but they did not think that it was a miserable or unhappy life. The monks were convinced that they had been chosen by God for this life together and so they were ready to obey the abbot, who was in many cases one of the family which had founded the monastery and so had a very special position in the history and tradition of the monastery. The founder-abbot was often related to a king or chieftain, and exercised an influence and an authority in the whole neighbourhood outside as well as inside the monastery walls. The monks obeyed the rule of discipline and also the rule of poverty, of upright, honest and well-controlled living. Their day was very strictly organised, but they looked on the rule as 'good discipline'. They were ascetic, 'in strict training', and so they kept themselves spiritually fit. Others called them 'the athletes of God'.

Among the communities of nuns, St Brigit was outstanding for her strong leadership and generous hospitality. She has been the inspiration of many other women's religious orders.

DIVISION OF THE DAY

Matins or morning prayer began in the dark! At two thirty a.m. the monks held a vigil. It was still early when the next service, *Lauds* or 'praises', was said between five and six in the morning, as the birds were welcoming the dawn with their song.Then at seven thirty came *Prime*, the first prayer of the day which had dawned at last. So far there was silence in the monastery, since these early prayers were said by the monks in their private cells; these early hours were also used for personal study of the scriptures and for meditation. The monks said prayers again at nine (*Terce*, the third hour after six o'clock sunrise) and at twelve noon (*Sext*, the sixth hour) and again in the afternoon at three (*Nones*, the ninth hour from sunrise).

Between nine a.m. and three p.m. much of the practical work of the monastery was done. The preparing of the main meal of the day, which would have been eaten after

Nones, the cooking of it and the cleaning of the cells and the other buildings occupied many of the brothers. Others worked on the farm and cared for the animals. Some said their prayers in the open air out in the fields, or on the river or out at sea if they were fishing.

Evening prayers (*Vespers*) were often sung. Some of the evening psalms 'before the ending of the day' suited this sunset time, just before the members of the monastery would 'lay themselves down in peace and take their rest', confident that the Lord was the only one who made them dwell together 'in safety and in unity'.

Some people have wondered if too many prayers were offered in the monastery. The monks would, however, look on prayer as a way of life. Just as breathing goes on all the time, so their prayers continued, without interruption, even when they were working with their hands, or copying the scriptures with their feathered quill-pens. To pray is to work, they said. To work is to pray, they added.

The monks were really specialists in prayer. They prayed more often than others because they were trained to keep silence, to use every minute of the day, and to concentrate on their life with God, *in* the world but, in another sense, in mind and outlook, not *of* the world. We learn about prayer from these specialists, but we would find it hard to keep up the high standard they set. We cannot all be explorers going in search of the North Pole, but we learn about geography and seamanship, about icebergs and strange fish life, from those who have risked their lives in finding out about some of these wonders of nature. We may not think that such long and difficult journeys are worth the time and money spent on them. Yet we now have more knowledge about the weather, the climate and the hidden resources of creation, discovered as a result of these special searches. We also benefit from the findings of spiritual explorers, who practise prayer, giving their whole time to it, in silence and alone-ness. They make discoveries about the spiritual life which help us as we try in a simpler way to speak to God. They can give us guidelines on how to start praying. The monks were doing research work. God was their project and the monastery was their university and their laboratory.

CHAPTER 3

Wandering Scholars

WHEN HIS TIME OF TRAINING for the sacred ministry of the Church came to an end, Brendan was ordained a priest by Erc, the bishop who had watched over him from the day of his birth.

Soon we find Brendan on the seas, sailing round Ireland, visiting the lonely hermits on their small islands and keeping in touch with many monks who shared a life of community together, beside lakes, or at the mouths of rivers, or on rocky headlands.

Columba (or Colmcille) was an outstanding personality of Brendan's time. In the *Life of Columba*, written by Adomnán (or Eunan), there is an account of a visit paid by Brendan to the island of Iona, among the inner Hebrides, off the west coast of Scotland.

Adomnán is one of the earliest writers to tell about

Brendan's adventures. He wrote: 'Four holy founders of monasteries crossed over from Ireland to visit Saint Columba, and found him in the island of Hinba.' This little island was not far from Iona. The four Irish visitors are named: Brendan is one of them, and with him on this journey were Comgall, Canice, and Cormac. They all admired Columba greatly, but Brendan, in particular, was deeply moved by the light that seemed to shine out of the great abbot of Iona. Adomnán describes the scene where the four visitors from Ireland are at worship together: 'Brendan saw a kind of fiery ball, radiant and very bright, that continued to glow from the head of Saint Columba as he stood before the altar.'

In the *Life of Brendan*, written much later, we learn more about Brendan's journeys to other islands off the Scottish coast. The meaning of the Christian's 'journey of a lifetime' seemed to unfold for him in his *currach* (*naomhóg*), a light skin-covered boat in which he wandered from place to place through these island waterways. He also visited Britain where he found much help and inspiration from Gildas, who wrote an early history of Britain. Here he learned fresh things about the religious life and the rules that were needed for the ordering and organisation of a monastery and its worship.

CHRISTIANITY – A TRAVELLING TRADITION

Christianity from the first was often described quite simply as 'The Way'. In the New Testament as well as in the Old, there were many descriptions of voyages. These travel tales had inner meanings. There was a spiritual message in the adventures of Jonah and the great fish that swallowed him. Jonah had to learn the hard way that he must obey God rather than follow his own wishes and choices. Jonah discovered on his ship's voyage that God loved everyone, of every race and nationality.

Abraham's journey inspired later travellers. There was a challenge in the call that came to him. He could not be deaf to it. He went out, not knowing where he was going. If he did not know the direction, he was inspired by the opportunity given to him 'to walk by faith', not according to any map. He sought a city 'which hath foundations whose builder and maker is God'. 'The city of God' conjured up a vision for the Irish travellers too, in the years that followed the collapse of the imperial city of Rome at the hands of the pagan invaders who sacked what had been so proudly known as 'the eternal city'.

Moses, another traveller, brought his people out from dark slavery in Egypt. They attempted what seemed to be a 'journey impossible', an Exodus, under his guidance. The Red Sea waters parted to make a path for them through 'a great and terrible wilderness'. Across this path they went until they obtained a vision of the promised land.

ST PAUL

The missionary journeys of the Apostle Paul made others see the importance of spreading the good news of the gospel from place to place. There was certainly excitement and risk in Paul's voyage to Rome, the capital city of the great empire. He reached the end of his journey although at times it seemed unlikely that he would ever come through safely. Paul wrote of his experiences afterwards to his friends in Corinth. In his letter to them he describes what he went through: 'Three times I suffered shipwreck, a day and a night I have been in the deep; in journeying often, in perils of waters, in perils of robbers, in weariness and painfulness, in watchings often, in hunger and thirst, in fastings often.'

We can picture the bravery of it all. This was the voyager speaking. He had survived tempests off the coast of Crete, when his ship, about to fall apart, had to be undergirded. The tackling had to be thrown overboard to lighten the load. The dangerous quicksands near Libya were narrowly avoided. For many days, neither sun nor stars appeared. The seafarers were obliged to drift 'up and down' in the Adriatic Sea, their ship out of control. They kept sounding the depth of the water, straining to keep off the rocks, casting four anchors from the stern, 'wishing for the day'.

Convinced that it was God's will that he should arrive at his destination, Paul inspired the crew, as they struggled on. He assured them that there would be no loss of life even if the ship would have to be abandoned and written off. 'Fear not', was his message, 'for I believe God'. All the vivid details of the voyage are recorded in the scriptures, and others, like Brendan, recalled the story as they set out on their spiritual journeys. It was important for Christians to know that, against all odds, the 276 souls on board, including Paul himself, landed safely.

If Paul could come through such dangers and difficulties, kept safe and protected by divine guidance, many another 'wanderer for Christ' also discovered the vital part which faith plays in such ventures out into the unknown.

The stories of these journeys in the course of the history of the Christian Church continue to fascinate us in our own day.

IRISH TRAVELLERS

PATRICK

St Patrick has been called 'a travelling man'. His memoirs, written by Tirechán, trace his itinerary through Ireland. So great was the impression he made on the people whom he met on the way, it seemed there was scarcely a corner in the whole island that he had not penetrated. His message filtered through. His presence seemed to be everywhere.

Ever since he made that journey to the sea-coast when he escaped from the slavery he had endured under a hard task-master, Patrick kept travelling on. A voice told him that his ship was ready. He voyaged out to a new life and a future that promised freedom. Another voice called him back after his time of training and ordination. He could not resist the invitation that cried out, 'Come, holy youth, and walk among us once more.' The voice of the Irish was heard, in a vision or a dream, by a Patrick who with a new confidence was ready to answer the call. People and places meant much to him; he loved Ireland and he had much to give to her people in the places where they lived. To this day his name is linked with mountains, churches, wells and towns. Croagh Patrick, Donaghpatrick, Patrickswell, and Downpatrick all figure in the long list.

COLUMBA

Columba was no less adventurous as a traveller. He kept in touch, by water and by land, with the communities which he loved to call his 'spiritual family'. Setting out from Derry for Iona, he may have appeared to be an exile, or a mere emigrant, banished or in search of a new start in life. In fact, he was much more like a missionary. He reached out to others to share the faith which gave him so much joy and strength. He sang songs in a loud voice that sounded far into the distance across the waters.

Columba established in Iona a famous centre of spirituality and study. Far from being a remote island, out in the blue, Iona was easily reached by ships from Scotland, Ireland and Iceland, not to mention the Faroe islands and Norway, and many other ports of Europe. Even from the distant Mediterranean, trading ships and pilgrim expeditions made their way. Monastic settlements east and west kept in touch with one another. A two-way movement brought enrichment and refreshment to the strict, well-disciplined life of the monks.

Iona was looked on as a centre of prayer and study. Many came to the island to learn; later they left Iona to spread the news of Christianity in all directions – north, south, east and west.

Ireland began to have a reputation for 'moving out'. The monks were men with a mission. Columbanus, who lived his active life at a later date than Columba, crossed over from Bangor in county Down to France. He took companions with him to help him in his task of reviving the spiritual life on the European continent. He and St Gall had both been trained for such work by St Comgall in Bangor's well-known monastery.

A boating-song composed by Columbanus as he and his crew rowed on the waters of the Rhine reveals the spirit of the expedition which brought Gall to Switzerland and Columbanus himself finally to Bobbio in north Italy, a town where he established an abbey and where he, as abbot, is today greatly honoured:

Lo, little bark (they sang)
on the twin-horned Rhine,
From forest hewn,
to skim the brine.
Heave, lads, and let the echoes ring.
The tempests howl, the storms dismay
But manly strength can win the day.
Heave, lads, and let the echoes ring.

Columbanus, with very good reason, wrote in a sermon (no.6), 'I am always moving from the day of birth until the day of death.' We can well understand why the day of the death of a saint was noted carefully in the records of history. Columbanus is remembered on his death-date, 23

November, and likewise Brendan's day is 16 May. Death did not mean the end for them; it was considered to be another move on the soul's journey, an entrance into the wider life, endlessly stretching out.

There are many lessons about life to be learned from these examples of voyaging and journeying. The physical energy needed to complete the course is matched by the spiritual excitement and the glorious anticipation felt by those who press on regardless. Some of the Irish pilgrimages and wanderings ended in experiences of happiness and states of blessedness. The travellers at the end of the day sensed that their mission was accomplished.

In Ireland, there were also many tales of voyages from ancient times, before Brendan's day. The voyages of Bran and Mael-Dúin were often described in story form. These voyage tales (in Irish *Immrama*) were very popular. There was exciting adventure to be looked forward to all the way through. Some lovely early poems were written and sung about these sea-journeys. One, translated by Kuno Meyer, puts us in the picture:

> Shall I launch my dusky little coracle
> On the broad-bosomed glorious ocean?
> Shall I go, O King of bright Heaven,
> Of my own will upon the brine?

Brendan linked himself with this spirit as well as with the Christian tradition.

A WANDERER FOR CHRIST

Brendan was 'a wanderer for Christ'. He set out to explore, not only because he had a love of adventure, nor because he was restless, looking for a change of place and occupation. He had a purpose in his journeying, and this becomes clear as we trace the happenings in his life.

Brendan was a missionary. His love for people and the great interest which he showed in them, when they were lonely and in need of help, made the journeys he undertook really necessary.

Also, he saw his life of faith and prayer as a pilgrimage. The more islands he visited, the more he learned about God's love for people and Christ's compassion for the suffering and the poor.

Christ's life, as told in the gospels, is seen as a journey. He himself went up to Jerusalem from the lake of Galilee. On the road, which was often stony and rough, more a track than a road, he met people in need, he cured them with a healing touch, he taught them and, in the end, he gave his life for them.

Brendan had been taught these things in his study of the scriptures. We can guess that in his mind, as he read the bible, the meaning of life's journeying took shape. In his meditations, written down centuries after his life, he recalled the events of the scriptures and of ancient Greek and Roman history. Many traditions are interwoven in his thought. The Odyssey of Homer, recounting the adventures of the Greek hero, Odysseus, who returns to his island home by ship after the long war with the Trojans,

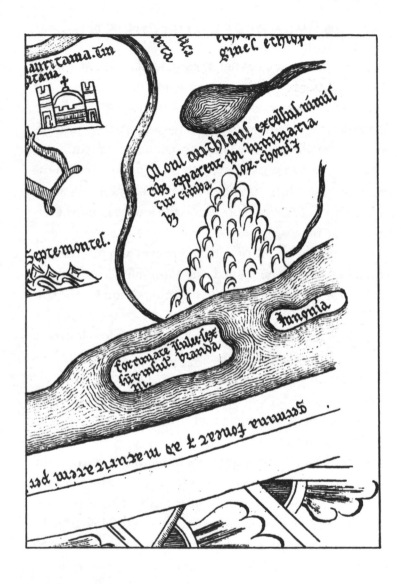

This section of the Hereford Map of the World (Mappa Mundi) *shows an island off the north-west coast of Africa, bearing Brendan's name* (Brandani).

has a human message not so very different from the journeys from exile and captivity experienced by 'the children of Israel', even if the faith behind the journey was of quite a different sort.

CHAPTER 4

The Voyage of a Lifetime

BRENDAN SEEMS TO HAVE BEEN A TRAVELLER from the very beginning of his life. He had an urge to see new places. Wherever he went, he made new friends. In his explorations he discovered more and more about the world.

He sailed around Ireland and visited many islands off the coast. The sea was in his bones. His name became well known in Scotland among the islands of the Hebrides. The fishermen still sing his praises. They have called rocks, harbours and headlands after Brendan. In their prayers, they thank God for a good and brave navigator who explored unknown seas and dangerous waterways.

Brendan sailed further still, to Wales and to Brittany in France. He brought back to Ireland much information about the life of the Christian Church in other lands. This experience helped him in his work at the monastery of

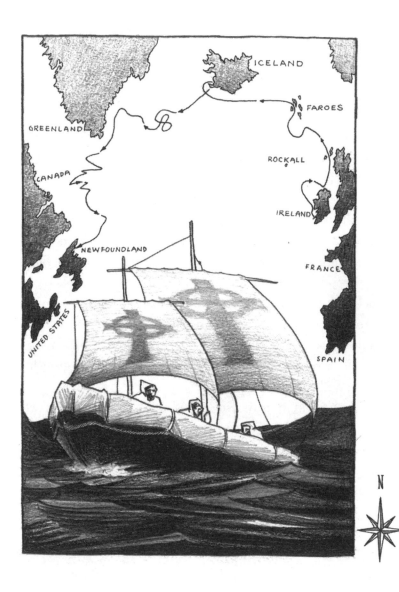

In the 1970s, Tim Severin built a boat like Brendan's and sailed off into the Atlantic. His journey took him to Iceland, Greenland and eventually to Newfoundland.

Clonfert in county Galway. Here in the quiet countryside, near the west bank of the great river Shannon, he was abbot in charge of a community of monks. He called them his 'family'. The members of the community spent each day in prayer, study, and handiwork of many kinds.

Brendan learned much from the personalities he met abroad. St Malo from Brittany in the northern corner of France had a special influence; he was also a seafaring saint. The harbour called after him faces the Channel Islands and is full of interesting historical buildings.

Malo was a cheerful saint. The Bretons tell stories about him as he rode on horseback visiting the towns and villages, singing psalms of praise with a loud voice. He also, like Brendan, loved to cruise along the coast. He looked on each island that he came to as a place of secrets and adventure. There was always something new to discover. If Malo passed on some of his cheerfulness to Brendan, we can be sure that Brendan filled Malo with a longing to travel and explore.

The 'Brendan trail' stretched into the continent of Europe, and his voyages may even have brought him to north Africa. There is a row of six small islands, named after Brendan, on a famous old map of the world. This 'Mappa Mundi', the Latin title of a 'map of the world', dated A.D. 1300, is one of the great treasures of the library of Hereford Cathedral in England. These islands off the north-west coast of Africa are not far from the Canaries.

It has also been noticed that on old maps an island called Brendan's Island has been marked on a spot far out in the Atlantic ocean, mid-way between Europe and the

Americas. However, this island does not appear on maps made in the past two hundred years.

THE GREAT JOURNEY

Brendan is best remembered for a famous voyage – the 'journey of a lifetime'. Many books have been written about this journey. It must have been the high point in Brendan's life.

Brendan heard in his imaginings, as he prayed, and in the dreams of his sleep, the call to launch out into the deep. He knew a great deal about seamanship. He was a skilful sailor, a clever boat-builder, and an experienced steersman who had navigated through some difficult channels and dangerously narrow waters. He had the confidence, therefore, to go out into the unknown. He also had a strong belief that there would be much to discover and learn about life on such a great journey.

His faith did not fail him. He had the feeling that God was giving him instructions to bring the good news of Christ's gospel into the wider world. He sensed also that he would find out what might be God's plan for his own life and his future. He was not afraid to set out for a place that was beyond the far horizon, further than the eye could see.

Today it is possible to be in touch with Brendan's great achievement. Tim Severin in recent years has amazed and delighted us with the story of his own voyage in his book *The Brendan Voyage*. Here he describes the trip undertaken by him and his crew. His voyage, begun on 17 May 1976, ended on the other side of the Atlantic in Newfoundland,

Canada, a little over a year later on 26 June 1977. The boat in which this adventure, 'the greatest adventure of the sea since Kon-Tiki', was experienced can be seen today laid up in county Clare at Craggaunowen. The wooden-ribbed framework, covered over with leather skins, is there for all to see. It was modelled on a boat used by Brendan. This boat gives the visitor a deeper understanding than any words can indicate of a very wonderful journey. Now at rest, it tells an exciting and most convincing story.

CHAPTER 5

On the High Seas

THE WHOLE IDEA OF A LONG JOURNEY westward seems to have started one evening when Brendan was having a conversation with his 'soul-friend' (*anam-chara*), Barinthus, who was looking sad. Brendan tried to cheer him up by asking Barinthus to tell him all about his wonderful experiences on a recent voyage he had made out to sea.

Barinthus began to speak: 'I had a son named Mernoc. He fled from me, because he did not wish to remain in the same place with me. He found an island called the Island of Delights near a rocky mountain. I went out to visit him and found him and many others living in community, happy and contented. Then my son Mernoc said to me, "Father, let us go in a boat and row out westward to the island called the Land of Promise of the Saints, the land which God will give us on the last day." '

One of the creatures who befriended Brendan and his crew at sea was Jasconius, a whale. They met him several times, and at first mistook him for an island. They celebrated the eucharist on his back! This is how a fifteenth-century artist drew these events.

Barinthus went on to describe this Land of Promise and he explained that it was, in fact, Paradise.

His friend's story made Brendan think very hard. He chose fourteen monks and told them of his plan. Brendan was determined to visit the place that Barinthus had described. The fourteen agreed to accompany him. Great preparations were made. They fasted forty days and then set out to Aran, to visit Enda, Brendan's friend and teacher. Enda gave the expedition his blessing and the whole crew sailed off to the Kerry coast where Brendan's parents lived. Brendan did not actually visit them, but he looked across lovingly from Mount Brandon (Brendan's mountain) to his birthplace.

THE BOAT

A boat had to be made ready for the journey. The monks made a coracle (*naomhóg*) or currach, using iron tools. The ribs and the frame were of wood. Some said it was shaped like a banana! The covering was tanned ox-hide stretched over oak-bark. The seams on the outer surface of the skin were then greased with fat. The crew stored some extra skins inside the boat. They took sufficient food for forty days out at sea and they also put supplies of fat and handy tools on board. They made a mast and a sail; and off they went with the wind and a prayer.

Three other monks who watched on the shore wanted to go with them and join in the pilgrimage. Brendan warned that it would not be an easy journey for them and then took them on board, with a warning of possible troubles. Two of them would meet with trouble, he said. But

The monks prepare their boat. A wooden frame is covered with skins just like the currachs of today. However, the monks added sails and covered over the top, making the boat seaworthy on very long journeys.

the third, a person of good character, would find great happiness.

THE DESERTED ISLAND

The crew were soon in difficulties when the wind dropped and they had to row. At the end of forty days, they sighted an island. After a long search they found a harbour and landed. No one appeared to live there. A dog met them and guided them to some buildings, all beautifully furnished inside. Food was already laid out on the tables. They said their prayers and went to sleep. For three days and three nights all their needs were provided for. They were tempted to take some of these good things away with them as they journeyed on. Brendan warned them that such daylight robbery would spoil the whole expedition.

One of the monks had, in fact, stolen a silver necklace. He owned up to his theft and was pardoned. But all was not over. The first crisis on the voyage occurred when, after receiving communion, death struck this guilty monk. He had been disobedient in spite of Brendan's warning.

Just as they were sailing out, a young man came with a basket full of bread and a jug of water for the 'long journey ahead'. These provisions would last until Easter. The monks had a meal every two days while the ship went 'hither and thither'. Then an island appeared and they found a stream full of fish there. There were sheep on the island too. 'Take an unspotted lamb from among the flock,' said Brendan to one of the monks.

A man suddenly appeared with food. He said it was an

honour to provide it. The day was Maundy Thursday. Brendan decided to celebrate Easter on this island. However, the man said that Holy Saturday could be celebrated there, but that Easter must be observed on another island just visible in the distance. The man added that in eight days' time he would bring further supplies, enough to last until Pentecost. On the nearer island they would stay until noon next day. Then they must go on to the Paradise of Birds and stay there until Pentecost.

THE PARADISE OF BIRDS

Brendan and his companions followed the man's instructions, and eventually, after much voyaging, they found an island completely covered with birds. There were whirring wings and clouds of feathers everywhere. The island looked like a bird sanctuary, a sort of Little Skellig, where flocks of birds roost and nest in safety.

One of the birds broke away from the great feathered army, and came to the ship. He made a perfect landing on the prow and balanced gently on the edge, his wings beating and creaking, making a bell-like sound. Brendan had a conversation with this bird. We wonder if he thought, as others at the time used to suppose, that these birds were really people who had died long before. Brendan's bird said that the whole flock of birds on the island was very happy to have escaped the disasters which had destroyed many other birds. These special birds had been preserved and they found that the island was like Paradise. The bird went on to say that on Sundays and holy-days they became human and sang songs of praise.

When the birds began to sing, so perfectly in tune was the chorus that their harmonies blended beautifully. These birds cheered up the crew with their music. To hear them chanting their praises of God out in the lonely ocean must have been very comforting for the monks who had worked hard and long rowing the boat and steering its course day and night.

'O sing praises, sing praises unto our King,' chanted the birds. Brendan felt God was very near to them. He received a message, through their singing, which informed him in what direction he should go. They told him also of the people whom he would meet.

So the monks departed from the bird-island. Flocks and flocks of birds accompanied them as they moved through the waters. Escorted for a short time by these feathered friends, all in the boat were delighted with this cheerful send-off. Some of the words they sang were addressed to 'God our saviour, the hope of all the ends of the earth, and of them that remain in the broad sea.'

Brendan said that the bird song was like food – something to remember and to be thankful for when they were far away from supplies, feeling very hungry and thirsty. He also said their songs were sweet as honey; the tunes and the rhythms helped the crew as they rowed the boat on days when there was little wind for good sailing.

A STRANGE ISLAND

The voyagers felt a little uneasy when they approached the dark, smooth, shiny surface of the next island. There was no sandy shore surrounding this unusual place. In

This is Jasconius, the fishy name given to a friendly whale.
The voyagers mistook his bulky form for an island.

fact, it was hard to make a landing. The whole black mass emerging from the water seemed to be very slippery. The ship drew up alongside. What kind of island was this? It was all very puzzling.

Not even one blade of grass was to be seen on the island. It had a stony look and was not very inviting. Brendan did not attempt to land. He stayed in the boat. Some of the crew, however, clambered on to the island and the morning eucharist was celebrated there. After their worship, the monks lit a fire with some of the drift-wood they had gathered and they prepared a meal. Some meat was put in a pot of water and soon began to simmer.

Then, suddenly, surprise! surprise! the island began to heave and to rise up and down like a great wave, churning in the sea. Panic-stricken, the crew began to shout and cry for help. Brendan rescued them and drew them into the boat. They looked back and saw to their dismay that the island had moved. The fire and the boiling pot could be seen about two miles away. The island had slipped off, lunging and plunging through the waves. Gathering extraordinary speed, it moved silently, with twistings and rollings that sent it faster and faster into the distance.

'Are you shocked by what has happened?' asked Brendan, when the excitement had died down. They admitted that they had received a terrible fright. Brendan then explained. He had had a vision the night before that this black hump in the water was not an island. It was a fish, very like a whale.

'His name is Jasconius,' Brendan went on with his story. 'He is always trying to bring his tail to meet his head. But

In this old woodcut, a monk finds shelter on the fish island.

he is so long that he cannot manage to bring the head and tail together.'

Iasc is the Irish word for a fish, and Jasconius is a grand and dignified name for this very large fish. Whales are the largest of those animals called mammals which include dogs, rabbits, and also human beings. The bodies of whales are protected and kept warm by thick layers of fat. They move about, migrating from cold icy water to the warmer seas of the tropics.

Jasconius appeared again in Brendan's journey, but the crew no longer felt afraid of this mighty fish which could have weighed more than a hundred tonnes. Friendly Jasconius helped to guide the Brendan boat to the Land of

Promise for which they had been searching. The stream-lined body of this majestic animal carved a way through the waters. Steering with his broad flippers, rather like front paws, he held his balance and directed Brendan and his crew at the end of their seven-year voyage. In this way, they reached the Land of Promise of the Saints.

Many more experiences were to come. Yet the moving of the whale-island was not quickly forgotten.

AN ISLAND OF MANY WELCOMES

Brendan and his crew had been sailing the ocean for three months without catching sight of any land. There was nothing but the sea and the sky all around them. They had just enough food to keep alive and had a meal every two or three days. They were feeling hungry and very lonely when suddenly they spied an island in the distance. At first they could not get very near it because there did not appear to be an inlet or a harbour. At last, after much searching they found a place to land.

Here they received a wonderful welcome. A man with a white beard met them with a friendly greeting and guided them to a monastery. All was silent within the walls, but the silence was such a welcoming one that Brendan and his companions felt immediately at home. Here was a monastery, much like their own Clonfert far away in Ire-land, but the atmosphere was different. The hospitality and the courtesies were more pleasant and relaxed.

The abbot, whose name was Ailbe, had come from Ire-land and was in charge of this island monastery far out in the ocean. He gave Brendan the kiss of peace and, with the

St Ailbe greets Brendan and his companions by washing their feet in remembrance of Christ washing the feet of his disciples.

members of the community joining in, he washed the feet of all the crew. That was a sure sign that, although there was a rule of silence, a loving welcome was extended to the new arrivals. With the washing of feet came the memory of Jesus washing his disciples' feet and encouraging them to 'love one another'.

It certainly seemed to be 'a home from home' for Brendan and the others after that lonely stretch on their journey. Bells were rung, meals were served in the refectory dining-room, loaves of bread were broken and shared, their thirst was quenched with refreshing drink.

The abbot explained that all in this community were well looked after. There was no hard work, no struggle to find food. The abbot said, 'Every day we have twelve pieces of bread, cut from two large whole loaves. But,' he told Brendan, 'on your arrival we have been given double rations! We have been here for eighty years. We do not feel any older since we came. We do not need any cooked food. Everything is supplied to us in a wonderful way.'

This seemed to Brendan to be the ideal life. He went with the abbot to the church. It was lit by seven lamps: three burned before the high altar, and two each were in front of the other two altars. Patens, chalices and cruets gleamed in the sanctuary. The voyagers joined in the worship 'before the ending of the day' and sang the psalms appointed for the office of *Compline*.

Brendan wondered if the rule of silence was possibly too strict and might become a severe strain on all who tried to observe it. The abbot said that there was such a thing as a friendly silence, and that quietness meant restfulness. He added, 'The only time we hear the human voice is when we are all together in choir.' The abbot was allowed to speak to guests and strangers, but the rest of the community kept the silent rule. The silence helped them to be happy and relaxed.

Brendan wanted to stay with them. He loved this place. Ailbe, however, said that God wanted Brendan to return to his own monastery in Ireland and to be buried there, when his earthly life came to an end.

Brendan did stay for Christmas and Epiphany. The abbot had pressed him and the crew to celebrate these great festivals with the twenty-four monks in the hospitable community of Ailbe. They would never forget the lighting of the lamps on Christmas Eve. A flaming arrow seemed to shoot through the window, piercing the dark and kindling all the altar lights. Like the burning bush on Mount Sinai, the candles were alight but never grew shorter. They were never consumed.

When all was wonderfully celebrated and the festivals were over, Brendan, with his men, set off again in their boat, sometimes sailing, sometimes rowing, until Lent.

AN ISLAND TO REMEMBER

One day as the monks continued on their voyage, a great pillar of sparkling crystal loomed up before their eyes. Its height seemed enormous. Like a lofty palace, with shining glass walls, it soared to the mists with clouds hanging over it.

In fact, this crystal vision was quite far off. It took Brendan and his companions a full three days to sail up close to this incredible island. It was not in any way an ordinary

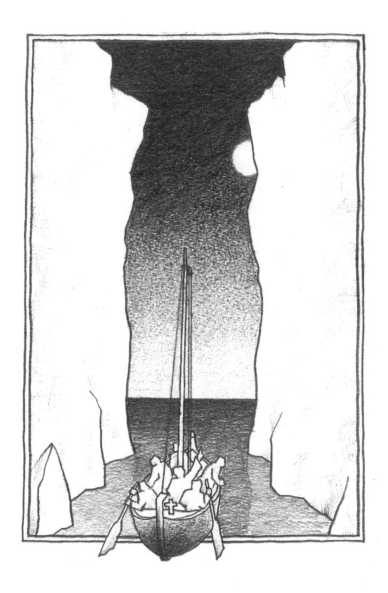

The sparkling pillar, soaring to the skies, strikes wonder into Brendan and his crew. The beauty and grandeur of God's creation was an experience never to be forgotten.

place. If a day's sailing brought the boat some 50-80 kilometres, the first glimpse of the crystal pillar was caught when they were more than 160 kilometres away from it.

If we met this massive column today, we would have guessed that it was an iceberg. In the Brendan story, we are told that something like a large net, described as a canopy, appeared to be wrapped round the pillar. The boat was able to pass through the openings made by the meshes of the net if the oars were shipped and the mast and sail were taken down. This net was silvery and finely patterned; probably each opening was six-sided. The description of this reminds us very much of an iceberg.

Icebergs are great chunks of ice which have broken off from an ice-cap on land. Glaciers, or great fields of ice, flow from these ice-caps and break in pieces as they move. Icebergs float and are carried along by the currents of the sea. Sometimes, they remain frozen for as long as a year. Naturally enough, they are a very real danger to ships passing near.

Mael-Dúin, on his earlier voyage, also met such a column. He was impressed by its silvery look. Brendan's story does not mention the word 'ice'. His description of the arches opening up for the ship to pass through suggest that the melting of the iceberg's surface had already begun. Those who know about icebergs mention that the disks that form when pieces fall off the iceberg, look in shape like a honey-comb.

There seems to have been a large gap, more than a kilometre in length, between the net and the 'crystal pillar'. This net, we are told, went down into the depths of the sea more than a kilometre.

Brendan let the boat move in through one of the meshes. The opening measured about 2 metres on each of the sides. The sea was as clear as polished plate-glass. The crew were able to see all that was happening beneath the water. They examined the foundations of the pillar and they saw the net lying in the sea-bed. For a whole day they sailed around the pillar, and even when they were in the dark shadow which it cast over them, they could feel the heat of the sun. Each of the four sides measured nearly 700 metres. They found a silvery chalice and a paten-like crystal all ready for use. Then they raised the mast and sail and the boat was blown along for eight days. There was no need to use the oars. All they had to do was hold the ropes and steady the rudder. God had given them a fair wind.

The monks felt that they had been in dangerous waters. Icebergs to this day are treated with great respect by seafarers. The great ship *Titanic* was wrecked after colliding with one of the thousands of icebergs which break off from Greenland and the Arctic regions each year. Some rise up to more than 100 metres above the surface of the water. In the depths of the sea below, they stretch hidden for over 300 metres and more. In 1912, only 705 passengers out of a total of 2207 on board were rescued from the *Titanic*, so dangerous were those drifting icebergs which blocked its passage from England to America. Those who survived that 'night to remember', like Brendan, were deeply thankful for escaping death and disaster.

A mighty, fire-breathing creature rescues Brendan
and his companions from the jaws of a monster fish.

CHAPTER 6

Towards Paradise

BRENDAN NEVER KNEW what he was going to find on the voyage. Sometimes the boat went in circles and covered the same waters through which he and his companions had already sailed. At other times, there were some new shocks and some pleasant surprises.

MONSTERS

A strange creature, stranger than a monster dolphin, was seen following them. It writhed and rolled in the white, foamy wake of the ship. It seemed to plough up the surface of the water, making even deeper furrows. It snorted and shot great fountains of spray from its nostrils. The voyagers felt threatened and began to pray in their panic: 'Good Lord, deliver us.' They thought of Goliath and felt overpowered by the monster's gigantic size. They thought also about Jonah and wondered if they were going to be swallowed up by this enormous fish-like creature. Great waves rocked the boat when this fierce sea-monster splashed about and churned up the waters.

Brendan's prayers were answered. The beast they feared so much met his match when another large creature of mighty strength attacked him. Flames of fire shot out from the mouth of the rescuing attacker, and the threatening monster was overcome and killed. He lay dead before their very eyes, afloat on the waves with his body chopped into three parts.

Later, when washed up on a nearby island, the crew made a meal of the beast they had so much dreaded. Brendan told them to salt one of the lumps of the dismembered body and keep it for the next stage of the voyage. The mighty, fire-breathing warrior, who had rescued them, had meanwhile disappeared into the mist. Brendan had had a lucky escape.

CHOIRS

Soon some more cheerful news was announced. The monks felt that God must have had some good reason for keeping them safe on this pilgrimage. On the next island they heard the singing of three choirs. The sound was beautiful and the harmonies raised up their spirits once again. This music suited the feelings and the mood of the crew after their journey in troubled waters. They heard the group of psalms called 'the songs of the steps' which were first sung long ago by the singers returning from exile, step by step, to their home city, Jerusalem. After many years of captivity in Babylon, these tired exiles had reached the end of their journey, and, by degrees, they came to a point on the road where the end was in sight; the towers of Jerusalem could be seen on the sky-line. Their songs have also been called 'the songs of degrees'.

'I will lift up my eyes unto the hills,' they sang. 'I was glad when they said unto me, Let us go into the house of the Lord.'

'When the Lord turned again the captivity of Zion, we were like them that dream,' was another song. 'Out of the deep have I cried unto thee, O Lord'. Those last words Brendan could also have sung from the heart, after his experiences among monstrous beasts. His crew seemed to be singing all day long on this cheerful island. Strangely enough, some of the pilgrim-psalms they sang sitting down and not while marching in procession. They probably felt that their journeying had come to a successful end. They had finished travelling, but the memory of it all stayed with them.

All through the afternoon, until the evening, the choirs lifted up their voices. The voyagers knew the words. They were reminded of the round of the day's worship in Brendan's monasteries of Ardfert in Kerry and Clonfert in Galway. The names of 'the hours' were very familiar; *Terce, Sext, Nones, Vespers* mapped out the day with the chanting of the psalms. Night fell and a white cloud covered the whole of the island. It had been a happy day. There were no more fears or frights. Next morning, what a joyful sound woke them up: 'O clap your hands, all you people; shout unto God with the voice of victory.' The old psalms really came to life on this island. They were now well prepared to receive communion.

Before they set sail for the next stage of the journey, the monks were given presents of fruit by the islanders. These fruits had a delicious taste - something very like honey lingered on the lips for a long time afterwards. But, as might be expected, a time of fasting came again, out at sea. However, one day an enormous bird hovered over the voyagers. He had a branch in his beak and from it he dropped bunches of grapes, as big as apples, into the boat. He was a most friendly and helpful bird, and soon, refreshed by the fruit he had brought them, they reached a sweet-smelling island, where the air was filled with the perfume of pomegranates, lovely juicy golden fruit about the size of oranges, for which North Africa is famous. Life was certainly sweet on this island.

THE GRYPHON

The sweetness was short-lived. The monks had not gone far on their way after leaving that pleasant island behind them, when an enemy attacked them. A strange creature, called a gryphon, (or griffin), suddenly appeared, flying through the air. They had heard about this animal but had never met anything like it before. They were reminded of a story about a flying object with an eagle's head and wings and the body of a lion. They were all terrified. Everything turned out happily, however, when their friend, the grape-bearing bird, appeared, gave chase and killed this nightmarish, weird apparition. The Brendan voyage had come through yet another danger spot.

The monks deserved a happy Christmas with St Ailbe.

This was how a fifteenth-century illustrator imagined the gryphon,
seizing one of the crew and, holding him fast with his sharp talons,
attempting to devour him.

In fact, the only proper rests they had during the long
years of their journey were at Christmas and Easter.

SEA CREATURES

St Peter's Day (29 June) was a festival celebrated on board
ship with the sea, like glass, calm and strangely solid-
looking on every side. The still water seemed to be so firm,
though liquid! It tempted those in the boat to step overboard and walk on it! Instead, they contented themselves

Brendan and his companions bravely face attack from the gryphon who hovers over the boat, poised for a downward swoop. Luckily, another bird comes to the rescue and drives away the frightening enemy.

by looking over the edge of the ship and peering into the green, clear water.

The sea was very deep at this point and the sun shining through the saltiness seemed to dance and play with its sparkling rays, making silvery patterns. The water was still and calm but the sunlight was full of interlacing, rhythmical streaks of glittering, quivering brilliance. These shiny shafts of light seemed to provide a musical accompaniment, quietly and very much in tune with the peacefulness of the deep waters. As they looked down, long and steadily, they saw teeming groups of sea-creatures. These animals (whatever they were - some think they might have been jelly-fish!) were lying, head to tail, on the floor of the sea-bed. They are described as appearing like flocks feeding in watery pastures, or, more vividly still, like a city on the march, moving with a gentle swell.

All on the boat were astounded at the sight. They suggested that a eucharist should be celebrated to mark their amazement at the hidden wonders of creation. They kept quite still and a hush fell on them, lest the scene should be interrupted. Brendan had quite a different view and began singing at the top of his voice. The fishy swarms, packed like sardines, were fascinated by the sound of his songs. They gathered round in their hordes, listening, but keeping a respectful distance from the boat.

THEY TRAVEL ONWARDS

One day, when the monks were feeling very thirsty as well as hungry, during the days of fasting, they saw to their delight a green island, with cool and shady shores and rocks in the background. They landed and soon found a sparkling spring gushing from the rocks. It was a tempting sight, but they were warned not to drink from it. They paid no attention to the warning and quenched their thirst. The result was that they fell into a deep sleep and did not wake for two or three days. This frightened them. They felt that they might not have woken up again, if they had tasted some more of this water. They sensed that they had been very near death on this beautiful island.

Off they sailed, a little disturbed by what had happened to them. That sleep had gripped them rather too tightly. The boat was becalmed for a while and they had time to think about the warning they had been given and their foolishness in paying no heed to the danger.

Then God sent a fair wind and soon, to their great joy, they found themselves approaching once more their 'Maundy Thursday' island. Here they had a bath and fresh clothes. They felt much better. They went off to the Easter vigil island and then set out for the Paradise of Birds, a familiar place they had come to love.

On the way, Brendan sang that famous song of the three brave young men who praised God with great faith and cheerfulness, although they had been thrown by their enemies into a 'burning fiery furnace' and had not suffered harm because God protected them. This song is called in Latin the 'Benedicite' because it opens with the words 'O all ye works of the Lord, bless ye the Lord.' It is a morning song. It praises God for the world He created and for all the wonderful sights and sounds on land and sea and in the skies above. We can well imagine how Brendan felt when he sang some of the words of this song. He must have admired the three young men who had refused to worship the golden idol as commanded by king Nebuchadnezzar. The three were loyal to the one true God and had to face punishment for their beliefs.

Bless the Lord, fire and heat. Bless the Lord, ice and cold ... frost and snow. O you whales and all creatures that move in the waters, bless the Lord.

The words spoke loudly to Brendan and his companions, after all that they had been through.

The birds sang a song of praise and greeting when they saw the boat arriving. 'Salvation to our God and to the lamb' they cried out in chorus. Long before the music of Handel's *Messiah*, those cheerful words from the Revelation of St John the Divine had been sung in praise of God's goodness. 'Blessing and honour, glory and power be unto Him ... and He shall reign for ever and ever.'

The Brendan story tells that one of the birds came to the 'boat-people' when they were at their meal. The bird made a noise with his shuddering wings and deep, throaty voice 'like some church organ'. He said to Brendan, 'God has mapped out four places for you - one for each season of the year. On Maundy Thursday, you will be with your steward who acts as your guide; at the Easter vigil, you will celebrate on the whale's back; from Easter to Pentecost, you will be among the birds; and Christmas you will spend with St Ailbe in his island monastery.'

Brendan comforts the monks while smoke and flames burst from the volcano. One has perished in the clutches of the threatening enemy.

The bird continued: 'After seven years, you will find the Land of Promise of the Saints. You will stay there for forty days. After that God will take you back to the land of your birth.'

A VOLCANO?

After a happy stay in the Paradise of Birds, Brendan and his monks set sail again. A strong wind carried them along swiftly, for eight days. They came at last to a barren, stony island. No grass or trees were to be seen here. The ground was strewn with black slag, which looked like charcoal clinkers. There was a grim sound of bellows blowing and hammers clanging.

'Let us get out of this place,' cried Brendan. 'The sooner we flee from here the better'.

A fierce-looking man appeared with a large piece of blazing, coaly clinker, held with a pair of tongs. He hurled this lump of fire at the boat in a most savage manner. It might have been a burning piece of melting lava from a volcano. Suddenly, the whole island was on fire. The sea hissed when the lava flowed into it and the hot stones shot out in all directions. The smell was foul. 'We are at Hell's gates,' shouted Brendan. It was a most frightening moment.

Then they met a high mountain, wreathed in cloud, which turned out to be smoke, belching forth from a crater-like opening at the top-most peak. This volcano opened its wide mouth and spat out hot burning streams of liquid lava. The cliffs of the mountain were black as soot. The face of the steep, sheer rock was like the wall of a

Judas, who had betrayed Jesus, was tortured by demons. Brendan feels compassion for unhappy Judas, and drives away the ferocious creatures who wheel around trying to snatch him away.

strong fortress. One of the three who had been taken on board at the beginning of the voyage met his death in this frightening place. He seemed to be drawn into the side of the cliff, by a powerful, fatal attraction. Unable to resist the pull of this magnet-like force, he perished in the intense heat. Brendan had foretold that this man would suffer. He, the last of the three who had risked the journey, was doomed. 'He brought this terrible judgement on himself,' said Brendan, who had known about the man's earlier life.

All the others sailed away at top speed. They looked back from a safe distance and saw the mountain still vomiting flames, which leapt up sky-high. The whole mass of the rock below glowed and glared like a huge bonfire, or, as the people in the boat probably thought, like an enormous funeral pyre, lit to cremate the dead.

JUDAS

After the volcano came another shattering sight. Seven days had passed and the monks were sailing along when suddenly they saw a strange-looking man perched on the top of a rock. He was wrapped in a cloak. Great waves battered this rock, just as wild seas in stormy weather dash against the little island of Rockall, many miles out from the coast of north Donegal in Ireland.

Was this a man, they thought, or was it an island? Perhaps it was really a ship and the figure on top might be a bird? They sailed nearer. They saw that here was a man indeed. His face was disfigured and he was evidently very miserable and depressed. He was covered with a wet sheet of cloth which smacked against his body in the whirling wind and stung his face and his eyes.

'Who are you?' they asked from the boat.

'I am Judas Iscariot, the one who bargained away his Master's life,' he replied. 'Because I betrayed Jesus into the hands of his enemies for the sake of thirty pieces of silver, I am being punished.'

Judas went on to say that he felt quite happy on this rock in the midst of the waves. He called the rock a 'Garden of Delights'. This was the place where he came to rest in between times of terrible suffering. Rest days for the tormented Judas were on the Sundays in the evening, between first and second *Vespers*, between Christmas and Epiphany, and again from Easter to Whitsuntide. He also was allowed to have this time of rest and relief on the festivals of the Purification and the Assumption of the Blessed Virgin Mary. But, for the remainder of the year, he told them, 'I am torn in hell with Herod, Pilate, Annas and Caiaphas', all the people who were involved in the condemnation of Jesus.

Judas said that his punishment was to be placed like a lump of lead in a burning hot crucible. This melting pot was 'in the middle of yonder mountain,' he said. This is the home of Leviathan, the huge sea-monster. There is a description of this creature in the Book of Job which would have been well-known to the monks: 'Out of Leviathan's mouth go burning lamps and sparks of fire leap out. Out of his mouth goes smoke as out of a boiling, seething pot or cauldron. His breath kindles coals, and a flame goes out of his mouth.' Judas said that he was there in the mountain when the third monk who had been with them in the boat was swallowed up.

Brendan was sympathetic and kind and felt much pity for Judas in his plight. He wanted Judas to stay on the rock until sunrise at least. He asked him what the cloth was for. Why was he holding it? Judas said that he had given it to a leper to comfort and heal him. He also said that the two bars he was holding were given to the priests of the temple. These bars were really spits or skewers on which meat was placed so that it could be roasted before the fire. The rock he was sitting on had been a stone that filled a pot-hole on the road. Judas had placed it there in his lifetime to help the passers-by to walk without stumbling. These reminders of the good turns which Judas did to help people gave him some relief after the long hours of pain and agony.

When night began to fall, demons came with threatening shouts. 'Keep out of our way,' they cried out to Brendan, 'we want Judas, we want to devour him as a tasty morsel.' Brendan replied: 'I am not the one who is guarding Judas. Christ is protecting him. I command you, demons, do not lay your hands on him.' In the morning, the demons poured curses on Brendan. They saw that he was a man of God. Brendan urged them not to torment Judas.

PAUL THE HERMIT

After that, Brendan sailed south, giving glory to God for all things, even the painful memories that they all carried with them. He learned from his time of prayer with God what new experiences they would have on their journey. 'You will soon meet Paul the Hermit,' he told the crew, as another island appeared.

They sailed round and round the shores of this island but it was very difficult to find a suitable landing-place. Then at last an entrance was found. Brendan tied up the boat. Coming ashore, he saw two caves, their open mouths facing each other. Here was a tiny spring of water and beside it sat a strange old hermit. He welcomed them all and greeted them with the words of a psalm, 'How good and joyful a thing it is, brothers, to dwell together in unity.'

This was Paul the Hermit who told them that he had been brought up in St Patrick's monastery in Ireland and had been the caretaker of the graves in the cemetery there. Paul saw that Brendan was a very special person, 'higher than any monk'. A monk has to work, but here was Brendan with his 'family of monks' who for seven years had been fed and clothed by God!

Paul told them about Patrick who had asked the hermit to bury him when the day of his death arrived. Patrick had given Paul further instructions: 'Go to the shore, find a boat, go to the place arranged for you and wait for the day of your death there.'

Paul sailed off for three days and three nights, and landed on an island. He then pushed his boat out to sea again with his foot. The boat drifted back to Ireland and Paul was isolated and alone, a real hermit. Yet he was never quite alone. He lived close to God and came to know him well, even if he did not meet other people. He was fol-

Paul the hermit had come from Ireland many years earlier.
We see him sitting outside his cave on a ledge of the steep cliff above the
waves. Brendan, after a difficult landing, receives a warm welcome and
much encouragement for his journey from this wise old man.

lowing in the tradition of the first hermit of all, who was also called Paul, and had lived a solitary life of prayer in the sandy deserts of Egypt.

The Paul whom Brendan met was very friendly and sociable. He said he had been a long time on the island. For the last sixty years he had existed without a mouthful of food! For thirty years before that an animal, an otter, had brought him fish for his dinner and some twigs. The twigs Paul used to light a fire. He struck a flint against iron and sparked off the flame which cooked the fish. On Sundays he filled a flask of water from a spring which trickled from the rock. This supply lasted for a week while each day he quenched his thirst. Paul said that it was only after a stay of thirty years that he discovered the two caves which Brendan had noticed. He said that he was fifty years old when he left Ireland and now he was 140!

This hermit was covered from head to foot with thick hair. He was quite well protected without any clothes. He was snowy-white all over and only his face and shining eyes could be seen. He was a wise old person. He told Brendan that there was a forty-day journey ahead of them on their voyage between that day and Holy Saturday. 'Go therefore,' he said, 'and fill your water-bottles.' He told the monks that they would travel to the Land of Promise of the Saints. They would be able to spend forty days there, but then they must return to the land of their birth.

THE PROMISED LAND

So the voyagers continued all through Lent on the ocean.

They were quite happy to have one sip of water every three days, so cheered had they been by the send-off which the hermit had given them.

They found Jasconius in his usual place and sang praises all night. After the morning eucharist they repeated the psalm they loved about God being the hope of them that remain in the broad sea. Then, in good heart, they set out again. The friendly whale helped them on their way. He swam steadily in a straight line and was their pilot. So they found themselves first at the Paradise of Birds, staying there until Pentecost. Then the birds wished them a safe journey as they steered their course to the Land of Promise of the Saints.

On the fortieth day, they found themselves in a thick fog. 'Do you know,' said their guide, 'that a dark misty fog surrounds the island you have been looking for during the past seven years? It swirls round and round the island.'

After an hour, a brilliant light shone through the mist and showed them a beautifully spacious island full of fruit hanging from the trees like apples in autumn. There were wells with a plentiful supply of spring water and a great river flowing through the centre of the island.

The monks were greeted by a young man who gave them all the kiss of peace, and called each one by his own name. He praised God and cried out: 'Blessed are they that dwell in this house. They will be always praising thee!'

The young man spoke to Brendan: 'You have been seeking this land all through these seven years. Jesus Christ did not allow you to discover it all at once. He wanted to show you many strange and wonderful things on your journey.

Fill your boat now with precious stones and return to the land of your birth. The day of your last journey is very near.'

So, home they went from this treasure island, enriched by the trials and testings of a journey of great faith and deep vision.

HOME

At first the return journey led the voyagers through a dark tunnel, a belt of fog and mist. Soon they came to the Island of Delights and after three days, with a blessing and a send-off from the abbot, they made their way at last to the home monastery near the Shannon river at Clonfert.

They received a wonderful welcome. Brendan told the community all that had happened on the long journey. He also said that he now knew that he was to die very soon.

It is thought that his very last days were spent in Annaghdown near Galway where his sister, Briga, cared for him. Two dates are given for the year of his death. The Annals of Ulster make mention of 577 and 583.

Robin Flower, who loved to stay on the Blasket Islands, off the Kerry Coast, wrote this poem about our hero, who has inspired many voyages of discovery through the centuries and continues to give much inspiration in our own day.

Sometimes I dream the whole rock-girdled island,
Adorned with the pale grasses and high ferns
And delicate faint-hued blossoms of the cliffs,
Floats insubstantial on the sea

Like the upthrust back
Of the huge fish Iasconius, where much-wandering
And far-adventuring Brendan held the Easters
Year after year of that long pilgrimage.
For this is Brendan's sea,
And yonder Brendan's mountain cloud-encompassed
Stands lonely in the sky ...

CHAPTER 7

Not Just a Tall Tale

LEGENDS AND TALL STORIES should not be lightly dismissed. More often than not there is some historical event or a genuinely hard-won experience at the heart of the story, passed on from mouth to mouth. Those who enter into the spirit of a great adventure describe the fears and the disasters in the colourful language of their own culture and personal background. The stories have a way of becoming more detailed and sensational when there is more time available for the telling of them. As one generation succeeds another, so the manner of expressing the point of the tale alters. If the event was terrifying when it occurred, the words used to describe it must surely be dramatic and arresting if the original shock of it all is to strike home. Tales told with artistry and passionate interpretation can convey the significance of a great discovery or a bitter calamity more fully than any

Brendan ponders the meaning of his wonderful voyage.
Fifteenth-century woodcut

bare chronicling of a historical fact.

In short, a journey can have several meanings. It may be an exile, an emigration, a pilgrimage, a mission, a spiritual experience with a vision of life's progress through the years here on earth and beyond death, or a way of worship, a devotional journey, a liturgical movement through the festivals and fasts of the Christian calendar.

We catch glimpses of life's journey in all its varying forms in Brendan's story. He is at once a very practical down-to-earth person, and yet other-worldly. He is a clever ship's captain, well-skilled in navigation. He is also a visionary and a prophet. What he encounters seems at first incredible, but later can be explained and described in the language of the physical world and its geography, and also adorned and picturesquely embroidered with a spiritual interpretation.

BRENDAN'S VOYAGE

If we set out on a journey, we think of the place which we wish to reach. We may consult a map and trace with our eyes or a pointing finger, the route we hope to take. We might measure the distance and guess how long we are likely to be on the way.

It is important, even on quite a small journey, to make sure that we know what turns to take, what landmarks to look out for, what difficulties we might meet. Among the many streets of a city, or out in the wilds of a mountain or misty countryside, we need to keep in the right direction and to know about our destination at the end of all our travelling.

Brendan's journey was not measured by any map, nor was it organised by a timetable. It was quite a different kind of exercise. We can see at least three separate meanings in his great voyage.

ADVENTURE AND DISCOVERY

First, Brendan and his companions undertake a challenging adventure with great seafaring skills. They make careful preparations before they sail out into the west and the setting sun. This sea-journey, often called Brendan's navigation, has become famous. Other sailors, explorers, and adventurers have been inspired by Brendan's great achievement. They have followed his example and, as a result, have often discovered new countries and unknown islands.

MEANING OF LIFE

Secondly, Brendan's voyage is described as a journey of life. The meaning of the saint's life is explained, as if he was from his first birthday right up to his death 'on a journey'. We read of the problems that he faces. He meets many dangers. He escapes from storms and shipwrecks. He comes across enemies who attack the ship. He also is wonderfully helped by many kind, generous people on the way. His faith gives him and his crew the strength and the courage to keep sailing.

It is not possible, of course, in this life-journey to trace on any map the places which he visits. The names of the islands describe his experiences: The Island of Delights and the Land of Promise and the Paradise of Birds are more than places on a chart or a map. They are part of Brendan's vision. With the help of this journey, with all that happens on the way, Brendan sees what life is for. His bravery and his hopefulness make his life with God closer. His faith is tested by these adventures, but grows stronger all the time. His life is made richer, more useful and more helpful to others. His example, even today, hundreds of years later, is followed by others who have been inspired by him.

This journey is not only a fine piece of navigation and

Brendan and his crew receive inspiration on this peaceful island
of the community of Ailbe.

seamanship. Quite clearly, it is a missionary journey. It is also a pilgrimage as Brendan wanders over the seas 'for Christ'. It is, in fact, a spiritual journey. Brendan found not only new countries, which had not previously been discovered. He found happiness. The treasures he found were not highly-priced pieces of gold, silver or jewellery. They were instead valuable spiritual blessings, such as wisdom, new knowledge, true faith, and the freedom that is found by living a good and honest life, spent generously in God's service with a caring love for all living creatures, including fellow human beings.

A WAY OF LIFE – A FLOATING MONASTERY

Thirdly, the journey was guided and given shape by the rules, not of navigation alone, but of the monastery from which Brendan had started. We read of the feasts and festivals, as well as of the times of fasting, which are celebrated out at sea by the crew. The prayers of the whole round of the Christian year are recited faithfully and regularly as they sail along. They follow the same pattern set by the prayers of the cloisters and the church within the monastery walls.

The travellers celebrate Christmas on one island, and Easter on another. They keep the fast of Lent and train, not only as oarsmen with hard rowing, but as monks who belong to a community, bound closely to one another and to God by prayers and psalms and spiritual songs. The long day is divided up. Every three hours they strengthen their lives and their spirits with prayer.

In the course of the voyage, they meet another community. St Ailbe, the abbot, welcomes them. They share the life of silence on an island out there far away from Ireland. They learn how the old abbot, now 140 years old, strengthens the life in his community and counts his blessings, since God gives to him everything he needs.

The monks loved the psalms in a special way. In some places they found that it was the custom to recite the whole book of 150 psalms each day. They spoke of praying the words of 'the three fifties'. In many places in the story of Brendan's navigation, written several hundreds of years after the voyage, there are quotations from these psalms. Some are psalms of welcome which they hear as they approach an island-harbour, like this one:

> Brother, how good and joyful a thing it is to dwell together in unity.

Other psalms have a real taste of the sea in their words.

> They that go down to the sea in ships and occupy their business in great waters … these see the works of the Lord and his wonders in the deep!

Endpiece

Brendan's name has appeared on the old ocean-maps. His story has been told in many languages. Brendan (or Brandon) island is marked in mid-Atlantic on the map, made in Portugal by Toscanelli in 1474, and used by Christopher Columbus. There is a Brendan Society today which seeks to encourage all the nations of the world to combine in friendship and peaceful co-operation with a Brendan-like 'outgoing spirit'. The stone carving at Bantry, County Cork, outlines a boat, like Brendan's, as 'he rows heavenward'. Many are the signs and traditions surrounding this famous navigator. He, who has inspired intrepid explorers to adventure for Christ, remaining humbled by his own experiences in

his dusky little coracle
on the broad-bosomed glorious ocean.

At the end of his life, he was still humble and not, in the worldly sense, at all boastful or proud of his achievement as he said: 'I fear the solitary journey by so dark a way; I fear the unknown journey to go before my King, the sentence of the Judge!'

MORE BEST-SELLING BOOKS FROM THE O'BRIEN PRESS

By George Otto Simms

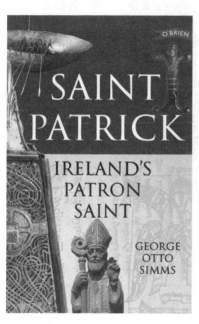

SAINT PATRICK, IRELAND'S PATRON SAINT

Illus. David Rooney

The real story of St Patrick, whose feast day is celebrated all over the world. Captured at the age of sixteen, this courageous young boy overcame many hardships to fulfil his calling: to bring God's word to the people of Ireland.

'Filled with ... superbly written insights into the real life of St Patrick.' *The Belfast Telegraph*

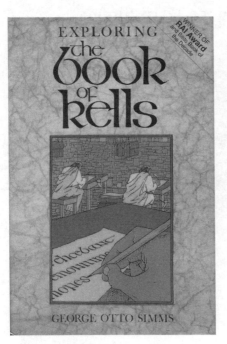

EXPLORING THE BOOK OF KELLS

Illus. David Rooney

Joint Winner Bisto Book of the Decade Award
RAI Special Merit Award

World-renowned authority on the Book of Kells, George Otto Simms, offers a compact, accessible guide to a national treasure. Fully illustrated and suitable for all ages.

By Morgan Llywelyn

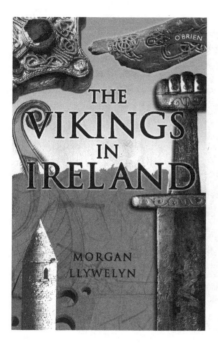

**THE VIKINGS IN
IRELAND**
Illus. David Rooney

Often seen merely as invaders, the Vikings were an important influence on Irish Art and Trade. This book is full of fascinating details about their way of life, with imaginative retellings of historical events.

By Mairéad Ashe FitzGerald

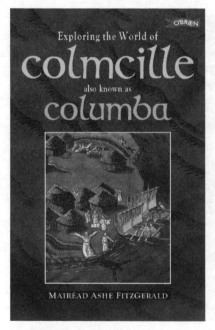

EXPLORING THE WORLD OF COLM-CILLE
Illus. Stephen Hall

A simple and accessible account of the life of this famous saint, who founded the celebrated monastery at Iona. Draws on history, art, literature and archaeology to tell Colmcille's story.

By Liam Mac Uistin

**EXPLORING
NEWGRANGE**
Older than the Egyptian pyramids, for 5,000 years the ancient Megalithic tomb at Newgrange in Meath has housed the remains of Stone Age 'aristocracy'. An accessible, fully-illustrated guide to the history of the tomb.

CELTIC TALES OF ENCHANTMENT
Illus. Shane Johnson / Russell Barnett

Four stories from the magical world of Celtic lore about the legendary Fionn Mac Cumhaill and the Fianna: 'The Enchanted Palace', 'The Quest for the Giolla Deacair', 'Oisín and Niamh Cinn Óir' and 'Ailne's Revenge'.

Send for our full-colour catalogue or check out our website